William Graham (signature)

Amoricon and Other Poems

WILLIAM GRAHAM

⚜

© 2008

Text © William Graham 2008.

All rights reserved. No part of this book may be reproduced in any form or by any means, electronic or mechanical, including photocopying, recording or any information retrieval system, without prior permission in writing from the publishers.

ISBN-10: 1-4196-9395-6
EAN13: 978-1-4196-9395-3

Interior formatting/cover design by
Rend Graphics 2008
www.rendgraphics.com

Published by:
BookSurge Publishing
www.booksurge.com

To order additional copies, please visit:
www.amazon.com

To Those Who Question

Part 1

Amoricon: A Verse Narrative

Prologue

Gather round the fire for it rains iron
Swords outside. The sky is low and dirty.
Stay warm—hear the tale of Amoricon—
A land found by searchers of purity.
Their gods sent them with a lofty mission:
"Leave behind your fields fertile and green.
Leave behind lodges for a land unseen."
Mothers wrapped their babes tight for protection.
From winds biting and rolling seas unkind.
This is a tale of hubris and of woe;
Many will die and not see tomorrow.
Many will fortune seek and become blind.
Sturdy souls will knock on the gates of death;
Other will feel light and take their first breath.

Canto I

1.
People are weak and desire to be led.
I have seen it with my own weary eyes.
They grab an idea as if it were bread;
Feeding their hunger, ignoring its lies.
There are always men with souls corrupted
Who use their visions to capitalize
On fear. Ladonus was such a leader.
Passion and hate he did equally stir.

2.
Reared on the barren plains of Rencelon,
Ladonus saw his mother and father
Combat the land like soldiers from the dawn
To the sunset. But nature would slaughter
Them, like a cougar preying on a fawn.
Harvests of sorrow rather than laughter
Stained the wretched childhood of Ladonus.
Bitterness infected his soul like puss.

3.
In the steppes below the Orak Mountains
That pierce the Rencelon sky like daggers,
Ladonus would find animal remains
Amid brush sucked dry by wind that swaggers
Down the cracked glaciers. White sheep skulls contained
Only dirt and rock—victims of cougars
That prowled steep escarpments. Ladonus swore
Not to be prey, but always predator.

4.
To his younger siblings three, he offered
This cool advice: "In nature, survival
Comes before family. Sharing bread
With me is foolish. I am your rival.
Look to yourself for sustenance instead.
Do not wait sheepishly for the arrival
Of a savior. He has abandoned us."
So to his own blood kin spoke Ladonus.

5.
Ladonus, wandering on lonely hills,
Came upon the homestead of Zakron,
Who survived, it is told, from self will
And cunning. Through the brush he crept along
Setting traps for birds and hares he would kill
For his food and simple clothing. Upon
His own strong experience he relied;
He would do so, he said, until he died.

6.
With white hair tangled like roots of a tree,
And an aroma like rotting red meat,
Zakron did not receive much company
In his small rural, ramshackle retreat.
On a cool morning in February,
To his astonishment, Zakron did greet
Young Ladonus, who confidently strode
Into in his cramped, decrepit abode.

7.
"Why do you disturb my solitude?"
Zakron asked. "I live among the rain,
The wind, the stars—not with the multitude."
Ladonus said: "I want you to explain
To me how a man can grow strong and shrewd.
Some say you are mad. I think you contain
The wisdom I need to escape the steppes;
To live, to die here, I will not accept."

8.
"I am ancient with no secrets to tell.
Let me live in peace in this wilderness."
"You were a leader in the capital,"
Ladonus said. "I want your grand success.
I dream all day and night of showing all
That from these barren lands I can progress
To the grand temples where people will hear
My words. They will then follow as I steer."

9.
"For a soft youth with no hair on your face,
Your ambitions fly high as a condor,"
Zakron laughed. "My sights are not commonplace
For one of seventeen years. My ardor,"
Ladonus said, "cannot be fast erased."
Zakron pondered this statement. "Your candor
Refreshes me. I have stories to share
Of the powerful and how they got there."

10.
"Let me tell you about wolf packs.
In each pack there is a dominant male.
He leads the pack through the woods to attack
Their prey. His will and his alone prevails.
He decides who can eat and who stays back.
Submissive ones unleash primeval wails
While the leader eats his fill of the kill.
Such are the just rights of the powerful."

11.
"The weak seeks the strong like the honey bee
Seeks flowers in spring. They need sustenance
From wise leaders who protect by decree.
Freedom gives many choices and chances
That people do not wish to take. You see
That the true test of savvy governance
Is to offer people the illusion
Of freedom but without true inclusion."

12.
Ladonus trekked through dreary autumn mists
And furious winter winds to Zakron's home.
After completing his chores, he would insist
On leaving his thick father's side to roam
Alone on empty trails. He would persist
In his dedication until he had grown
Sufficiently wise to shape his future.
Power for him had the sweetest allure.

13.
In his eighteenth year, Ladonus informed
His parents that he was leaving the farm
For the far capital Tulin. Alarmed
At his bold words, his parents warned that harm
Would be his sad destiny. "Be forewarned,
Foolish one; city vultures always swarm
Around those alone and unsuspecting."
Ladonus laughed: "People will feel my sting!"

14.
Leaving behind tears staining the faces
Of his family, Ladonus toward
His future walked. In his heart were no traces
Of remorse or sorrow. His ambition soared
As he imagined Tulin's grand spaces.
Zakron told him that there his reward
He would construct. Alone under the stars
He conjured the cheers of his followers.

Canto II

1.
Solitary Ladonus hiked down
The steep valley of the Dorlon River
Toward Tulin. To a man of renown
He would a note from Zakron deliver,
Ensuring he would soon be surrounded
By mighty people whose decisions confer
Favor, fame, dishonor on friend or foe;
That is, when they give thought to those below.

2.
The road to Tulin was ragged and rough.
Bandits lurked in hills above the river.
One night, three rogues descended from the bluff
And ambushed lone Ladonus, who shivered
With cold and fear. "Give us your bag," a man gruff
And smelly ordered. "There is nothing there
Of value. I am a poor traveler.
You can tell from the old clothes that I wear."

3.
"Your clothes too shall we take," a bandit said.
The three men beat and battered Ladonus,
Leaving him naked. Blood flowed down his head.
He crawled on sharp, cold rocks, barely conscious.
Without food and warmth, he would soon be dead.
He thought: "No person ever will I trust."
Tired and torn, he fought to stay awake,
Wondering if his trek was a mistake.

4.
Rain spat on his head as night smothered day.
He spotted a small cave under a ledge.
He piled small stones to keep the wind at bay.
"I will have my raw revenge; that I pledge,"
He said, shaking. Fear he would not display,
But pain and hard cold pushed him to the edge
Of sanity. He bellowed angrily—
Unsure if the next sunrise he would see.

5.
Ladonus awoke to find a sheepdog
Sniffing him suspiciously. "Who are you?"
Asked a girl, obscured by morning fog.
"I am cold." To Ladonus she threw
A blanket. Another unplanned prologue
To his mission, he thought. "I must thank you
For your kindness. I feared my death was near.
My hope was waning, and then you appeared."

6.
"May I know your name?" The dog growled as he
Stepped forward. "I am Ladonus, a victim
Of bandits. I have nothing left you see."
"Stay where you are. Don't move. I am Gulwin,
Daughter of Enral. This is our country."
"I mean you no harm. My head pounds. My limbs
Are bruised. All I seek is some warm dry clothes,
Food and drink. Will you provide me with those?"

7.
Gracious Gulwin bid him to follow her
Without saying a word. Ladonus saw
Her golden long locks like a chandelier
Glowing softly. Her silk skin had no flaw.
As the sun soared high, the fog disappeared,
Revealing a grand sight that gave him pause—
For below was a vast verdant valley.
Ladonus stopped to gaze at its glory.

8.
Gulwin led him down a trail to a house
Warm and inviting. A fire blazed brightly
In the hearth, next to which an old man drowsed.
Gulwin whispered in his left ear gently.
His eyes glared sharply at Ladonus.
"You are in need of warm clothes. Follow me,"
He said. As Gulwin prepared the morning
Meal, her sad heart began to dance and sing.

9.
Ladonus dressed in clothes that were too small.
Even bloody and bruised, his rugged face
Entranced Gulwin. To them, he did recall
His trials on the trail. "Quite disastrous,"
My boy," her father said, "that you did fall
Victim to such a fate. This is no place
For a young traveler to venture alone.
My advice is to heal, then return home."

10.
"I cannot return," Ladonus explained.
"I must continue to Tulin. For there
I am long expected. For there, I trained."
Gulwin replied: "Tulin cannot compare
With the bounty and beauty here contained
In our valley. Stay and breathe this sweet air
With us." Ladonus smiled: "Your invitation
Is kind. But I must keep my direction."

11.
Gulwin hung her head in disappointment,
For she longed for a handsome companion
With whom to roam the hills in contentment.
Ladonus maintained his dedication
To his quest. No fair maiden would prevent
Him from arriving in Tulin. He shunned
Love. After resting for just two short days,
He left, heading for Tulin in the haze.

Canto III

1.

Ladonus paused to catch his breath—below
Him on a wide grassy plain sat Tulin,
Towering in stone with windows aglow
In the molten blaze of late afternoon.
Through the city gates into a fast flow
Of humanity he went to begin
His search for Senator Lawdor—the man
Who could assist him with his fevered plan.

2.

He asked directions to the senate hall—
A stately edifice of carved marble
And statues of leaders past. On the walls
Hung thick tapestries of epic battles,
Where generals conquered enemies all.
Arriving at Lawdor's chambers, he pulled
Open a heavy oak door. "I am here
To see the senator, whose renowned career

3.

Has inspired me to travel distances
Severe, and suffer gross indignities
Just to meet him here." "The senator has
No time to waste with a boy. He only sees
Men of equal stature. You do not impress
Me with your rustic clothes," a secretary
Scoffed. "Tell the senator that a student
Of Zakron is here. From him I was sent."

4.
The man laughed at Ladonus' insistence.
"Right this way, sir. I am at your service."
Lawdor's chambers suited a man of substance—
Plush and elegant. "Let me be concise,"
He said to Ladonus, "Give me the sense
Of your visit here." For thirty minutes
He spoke of his apprenticeship with Zakron.
"Your mentor from society has withdrawn."

5.
"He lives in a filthy hut on the steppes.
He has lost his nerve." "But did he not train
You?" Ladonus said. "He taught you concepts
Of power that have marked your granite reign
In the senate." "You speak smoothly; no missteps.
"You have learned well. But you cannot remain
In those rural threads if you are to be
Seen with me. Appearance is destiny."

6.
Lawdor groomed Ladonus to his liking;
Gave him a suite of rooms in his sprawling estate,
And began to show him what power can bring.
Taking the lead in a senate debate—
His vote assured after taking offerings
From local merchants—Lawdor berated
People promoting shorter working hours:
"What will they do with extra time? Plant flowers?"

7.
Lawdor scoffed. Laughs flooded the chamber.
Each week, Ladonus collected grand gifts—
Coins, jewels, artwork—fit for a connoisseur.
In return, Lawdor's patrons received swift
Passage of laws. A keen entrepreneur
With a taste for high living, Lawdor sniffed
About Tulin's beautiful boulevards
Like a fox looking for hens in barnyards.

8.
Ladonus quickly gained a reputation
For his ruthless devotion to Lawdor,
Who enjoyed witnessing the formation
Of a fellow first-class power broker.
Ladonus displayed no trepidation
For doing tasks that others may abhor.
From soliciting bribes to cracking heads
To telling lies, he was a thoroughbred.

9.
Ladonus relished his new-found stature.
At Lawdor's soirées, comely women
Floated across the room for him to lure
Into his bed. Tears flowed time and again
From their eyes as new loves he did procure
To replace them. "Do women soil your den
With their lace and perfume?" asked Tamar,
Lawdor's wife. "I observe you from afar."

10.
"The sweet pleasures of their company fade
When their faces become too familiar,"
He said, smiling "I do not masquerade.
I am not their dear devoted lover."
Tamar replied: "Do you plan to evade
A woman's enduring love forever?"
"My dalliances will never be through
Until I find a mate as strong as you."

11.
"I am the wife of your wealthy patron.
I could tell him of your shameless flirting."
"But you will not," he said. "You will not run
To him because he is old and boring.
I am who you favor. I have begun
To see it, Tamar." "A sweet tune you sing
Into my ears. You see how much I yearn;
But Lawdor is a dangerous man to spurn."

12.
"Anyone call fall. We can rule together,
Or you can remain in his bed of stone,"
He said, reaching for her fiery hair.
"Ladonus, you will not leave me alone
Like the others to wallow in despair?"
"Never. Lawdor's house will be overthrown
Only through our passionate alliance.
In strength and love we must have reliance."

WILLIAM GRAHAM

Canto IV

1.
After gaining a passport to her bed,
Ladonus devised plans to eliminate
Tamar's husband Lawdor. "Brutal bloodshed
We must avoid. We must now concentrate
On a subtle plot containing no thread
Of suspicion pointing to us. Mistakes
In preparation will lead to our death.
I am not ready to take my last breath,"

2.
Ladonus said. He fulfilled his duty
Without change, but he secretly contacted
High Priest Albon, a vocal enemy
Of Lawdor's earthy excess. "He will dread
The day of judgment. Anyone can see
That he serves only himself," Albon said.
Shrewd Ladonus observed the potential
In Albon—Lawdor's death would be God's will.

3.
"Like a wasp, my conscience stings me each day,"
Said Ladonus. "I seek the salve of God."
"To find God's forgiveness, first you must pray,"
Albon said. Ladonus' devout façade
Fooled Albon. "It takes little to betray
The holiest of men. But to his squad
Of believers I will feign alliance
Until in time to my tune they will dance."

4.
Albon vowed to support Ladonus' plan
To force Lawdor from his senate power.
Trusting Albon did not know that the man
He so despised would soon be devoured
By Tamar's schemes and her lover's rough hand.
"The time is near when bouquets of flowers
Will be laid at dear Lawdor's stately grave,"
Ladonus said. "We shall have what we crave."

5.
Tamar heaped much tenderness on Lawdor,
Igniting his senses through the hot nights.
"The heat stifles. I long for the cool shore
Where sea breezes swirl against cliffs. Delights
Such as these when Tulin burns I long for,"
She said. "Let us from the city take flight
To your home on the heights of the sea coast."
There, she thought, he will slide from man to ghost.

6.
At Lawdor's lavish seaside home, Tamar
Ordered the servants away for the night.
She suggested that he smoke his cigar
As they strolled the path on the rocky heights
Overlooking the shore. "The flood of stars
Above is magnificent. Such a sight
Has enthralled me since I was a boy,"
He said. "I am pleased that I can enjoy

7.
This evening with you—whom I hold dear."
As he gazed up again to the heavens,
Tamar pushed him in the back with no fear.
He stumbled; then he made a fast descent
Into the darkness. She shed no false tears.
She returned to her bedroom. "The ocean
Is his chamber tonight," Ladonus said.
"You have done well. Now come to our warm bed."

8.
Ladonus departed before the dawn.
When the servants returned, a search began
For Lawdor. Weeping Tamar had withdrawn
To her room. Lawdor's crumpled corpse was crammed
Against the rocks in the surf. "He is gone,"
Tamar moaned, as a young widowed woman
Was expected to do. "His tragic fall
Leaves emptiness in the hearts of us all."

9.
Through Albon's influence, the prime minister
Appointed Ladonus to take Lawdor's seat
In the senate. Any talk of sinister
Plots was squashed. No evidence of deceit
Was found. Ladonus beamed as the transfer
Of vast power to him was made complete.
At the state funeral, his oration
Signaled his intent to lead a nation.

Canto V

1.
Ladonus solidified his power
By invoking God's word and tethering
Himself to Albon's church. "Now it is our
Time—the time of the righteous to here bring
Forth a new government that will tower
Over the past's corruption. We will sing
The praises of the Almighty and vow
To let his holy doctrines lead us now."

2.
The coalition that Ladonus forged
Swept in many laws like a hurricane
Forces the seas onshore in a strong surge.
All commerce moved to the church's domain.
High ambition and holiness converged
In Ladonus, but his true tastes remained
Out of public view. "Let them see me pray,"
He laughed. "What they believe I will display."

3.
To Tamar's fiery bed he returned
Each night. It was too soon, he said, to show
The world their devotion. "I now have learned
That our enemies are hungry to know
More about Lawdor's demise. I am concerned
They will cause use grief. We must forego
A public announcement of our engagement.
Our pairing others may misrepresent."

4.
Across Rencelon Ladonus stirred crowds
With his skillful message of deference
To powerful leaders. "You should allow
Us to chart the true course. We have immense
Knowledge of laws and scripture. We all vow
To do what is right. This burden intense
We gladly bear so that you can live free
Of want and fear. On this we shall agree."

5.
Dissenting voices began to murmur
In homes and public halls of Rencelon.
From the fields came a provocateur—
Strong-willed Darsen—one who dared to question
The motives of church and state. "I prefer
Not to abide by such a concession
Of rights and common sense," he said. "What they
Call freedom is really freedom betrayed."

6.
Darsen lectured to all who would listen
Of the empty eloquence of Albon
And Ladonus. "Their sordid mission
Is to dazzle and deceive. They are con
Artists. We must be in opposition
Or a loss of rights will be a foregone
Conclusion." His strident words began to
Make him a person who must be subdued.

7.
Shop owners forced to pay inflated rents
Protested with small landowners in towns
Across Rencelon. They hoped to torment
The prime minister—puppet of Albon
And Ladonus—and his false government.
"Darsen is acquiring too much renown,"
Ladonus warned. "Those unschooled in the ways
Of power—a steep price they shall now pay."

8.
"The unlearned seek to disrupt God's holy
State with their demands. Forcefully we must
Strike hard righteous blows against enemies
Of our land," Ladonus said. "We the just
Must not allow the unjust to decree
To us. They are not the chosen. Robust
Will be our response. Let no man wonder:
We will unleash our lightning and thunder."

9.
Soldiers fanned out across the land to crush
Those opposing state laws. Neighbor betrayed
Neighbor for a few gold coins. Spears were thrust
Through chests and necks. Severed heads were displayed
In squares, blood dripping on cobblestones. Disgust
Filled not the hard hearts of soldiers; they prayed
For glorious battle. No tears they wept
As on corpses of the vanquished they stepped.

10.
Ladonus and other senators saw
The aftermath of a bloody skirmish
In the sweet Dorlon valley. The sight gnawed
At some for many nights. Gutted like fish
Were women and children. "We must withdraw
Our forces. This is savagery. I wish
We had never started this vile slaughter,"
One senator said. "Evil now reigns here."

11.
"The deaths of innocents sometimes occur
In crises such as ours," Ladonus said.
"But let not this woeful tragedy blur
Our judgment." Just then among the dead
He spied a frozen face that he was sure
He knew. He kneeled and wiped mud from her head.
Gulwin it was; her golden hair now brown.
At her he gazed until the sun went down.

12.
In dawn's light he found her father Enral—
Cold and stiff. He ensured that they would burn
Not in the pyre. Hard rain started to fall
As he buried Gulwin and Enral—returned
Now to their land. Back in Tulin, a pall
Descended on his heart. His chief concern
Was altering the course of cruel events
That now raged. A new scheme he must invent.

Canto VI

1.
Darsen's capture and imprisonment reduced
Tension in the land. Yet young Ladonus
Grew weary of battles won that produced
No satisfaction. To his surprise, disgust
Was what he now felt. Power had seduced
Him; now he must find a cause he can trust
Again. He recalled Zakron's instructions:
"Focus people on noble distractions."

2.
Ladonus scoured the shelves of the state
Library. He found a small musty tome
That described Amoricon—land of great
Forests and rivers where large wildlife roamed
Abundant; a land where men could create
A grand city on a hill to call home.
He would embark on a journey to see
If Amoricon was fact or fantasy.

3.
Ladonus told Tamar that his vision
For a long journey to far Amoricon
Would be fulfilled. "Your grand decision
Sounds dangerous," Tamar said. "You act on
Legends of a distant land." "The reason
I must depart is clear: I act upon
God's words. Amoricon does exist.
On our voyage, God will be in our midst."

4.
To astonished colleagues Ladonus announced
His resignation from the senate's halls.
"I have a new calling. I have renounced
My prior path in life. Heaven's voice called
And I have answered. With every ounce
Of strength I have inside, I will lead all
Who choose to follow me to Amoricon—
To raise their fair daughters and able sons."

5.
Throughout Rencelon, people turned their thoughts
From civil unrest to the decision
Of Ladonus to lead a voyage fraught
With danger. Many expressed derision.
It bothered not hard Ladonus. He sought
Investors in ships and their provisions.
To some, he made promises of profit;
To others, salvation was a better fit.

6.
People were willing to take a journey
To the edge of the vast unknown—inspired
By the promises of a man of twenty.
"Zakron's teachings proved true: All they require
To follow are words from a deity—
They are silent sheep; I am their shepherd.
Dear Tamar, our ship embarks tomorrow.
In six months more, another will follow."

7.
A shipped called *Providence* set sail in May
The plan of Ladonus to rule a new
Land would soon come to pass. "I must display
Confidence in this endeavor. My view
Will be fair winds and calm seas to allay
Fears and doubts of the passengers and crew."
To show hope, the captain married Ladonus
And Tamar—a union all could see was blessed.

8.
The passage across the Arcturan sea
Was perilous. Wicked west winds whipped
The ship strongly. People prayed for mercy.
Many of the young and infirm perished.
Reaching Amoricon was not guaranteed,
People whispered. All dreams that they cherished
Would sink like stones beneath the cold, cruel waves.
Saddened, they dreaded a watery grave.

9.
"When will we see the shore of Amoricon?"
They pleaded. "We are growing desperate
To see land. Each day, all we spy upon
The horizon is endless sea. Our state
Of health is poor." "The miles have been hard won,"
Ladonus replied. "But our glory awaits
Us over the horizon. To me God
Has spoken. On dry land soon we will trod."

10.
After forty days, the crew spotted land.
Amoricon was not a mere legend;
It was real. But Ladonus had not planned
To encounter such bleak terrain. Ascend
They must formidable black cliffs to stand
On flat ground. The pilgrims had to amend
Plans to found a city on this brown plain.
Ladonus could not yet begin to reign.

11.
Food was scarce and the low black sky spit ice.
"Where are the forests and the swift rivers?"
People asked. "This is hell; not paradise."
Disease struck down the old; newborns shivered
In the cold. "God asks us to pay a price
Too dear. Ladonus, you must deliver
Us from this penance." Ladonus spoke slow:
"There will be a path, a sign. That I know."

12.
The words of Ladonus failed to inspire.
Within the rude camp, starving mutineers
Gathered in the bitter night. They conspired
To kill Ladonus and his Tamar so dear.
They tied them to wooden posts near a fire.
"We won't let you lead us to our deaths here.
Those of us alive to home shall return,"
Their leader said. "The two of you will burn."

13.
"You dare to challenge me!" Ladonus yelled.
"Only I know the path to vast riches
And salvation. Others will come to dwell
And reap the rewards that you now itch
To cast aside. To your souls say farewell—
For you will be eternally damned and pitched
Into hellfire!" His people laughed. As the flames
Shot high, the condemned spoke each other's name.

Epilogue

Dawn's rosy cheeks peek over the far hills.
My sad tale of Amoricon nears its end.
People went insane and perished until
Amoricon's stone silence returned again.
Deliverance, the second ship, did sail
To those distant shores. The emigrants found
No traces of life. But they heard the sound
Of lovers' cries. They searched to no avail.
They saw no life. The bare land was haunted,
They thought. "Before we succumb to a fate
We dare not think, we must leave or await
Our demise. This dry land our daily bread
Will not give." Providence guided them home.
No more from Rencelon did people roam.

Part 2

Theater of Ice: Poetical Vignettes

WILLIAM GRAHAM

THEATER OF ICE

I traveled so far I did not think
I would arrive at the theater of ice.
Illuminated by austral light,
No music or dramatic monologues
Fill the house—only arias
Of immaculate snow that boom and then
Are swallowed by unforgiving waters.
Immune from critics' parlor judgments,
Performances in this theater have open-ended
Runs—until the crack of doom opens.

Antarctic Midnight

At the bottom of the world at midnight,
The twilight undressed like a French coquette,
Revealing seductive light to delight,
As the sun performed a polar pirouette.

Celebrity Cruises

Once while on a stately sailing ship,
A woman asked me at cocktails and schmoozing:
"I hear you are a writer of some renown."
I replied: "No to the adjective; yes to the noun.
For writers, Madame, are mostly anonymous.
But that you've heard my name is a plus.
The truth is my verses are an acquired taste."
With that, the woman departed with great haste.
For on the other side of the long wooden bar,
Stood the great, great third cousin of the last Russian Czar.

Books on Board

Locked behind glass cases like specimens,
Sat books discarded by women and men
Who had taken this journey before me.
Their tastes ranged from the hard-boiled mystery
To the trench-coated political thriller.
Like me they would read and then pause to stare
At the sea and the sky sliding softly by,
Longing for when they would no longer comply.
Maybe hoping for the sweet taste of intrigue
Before succumbing to age and fatigue.
On long voyages you have time to dream
Of your plans and plots and what might have been.

Buenos Aires

Sprawling jewel of Argentina,
Will you ever be known for more
Than the tango? It must bore
You when touristas think that a

Trip to a high-priced tango show
Means they have discovered your soul.
No. They must venture out and stroll
Slowly on tree-lined streets to know

The real Buenos Aires—city of parks
And cafés splashed with southern sun.
When tourists are asleep, true fun
Starts—after midnight, sexual sparks

Fly in hot clubs until the dawn.
Dripping and drowsy, locals return
To their homes to cool down the burn;
Then head to work, stifling a yawn.

Cape Horn

He dreamed of Cape Horn
Since reading a story torn
From a Boston newspaper.

Sleek sailing ships plied the rough
Waters, manned by old salts gruff
And hard from New England.

He climbed trees, straight as poles,
Pretending to see the whole
World from the topmast.

The gold rush gave him the chance
To work on a ship called *The Lance*,
Heading from Boston to San Francisco.

As the ship neared the cape,
A storm blew, from which there was no escape.
The young lad was adopted by the old mad sea.

His mother received a letter of condolence
From the ship owner in Providence.
She then could no longer bear the sound of waves.

Southern Cross

Was it polar madness
That drove them to the south?
Or exquisite sadness
That tainted their clear youth?

Under the midnight sun
They stepped on the sea ice
Without telling anyone.
The landscape did entice

Them to misplace judgment.
Their bodies were swallowed—
A tragic accident.
A cross now shows ground hallowed.

How long did mothers weep?
Is an eternity
Enough time to keep
A face in memory?

The Naked Truth

The Spanish found the natives of
Tierra del Fuego walking naked in the forest.
They plunged into frigid water and
Copulated without care in glacial winds.
When the Spanish gave them clothes.
They died. Now their last remaining
Ancestor lives in a government house
Near the airport. She requested to be
Buried with no clothes on.

Pure Cold

Pure cold splinters the air,
Sending shards of sky into your face.

Pure cold thrusts a spear in your chest;
The victim—your breath—floats with spectral grace,

Leaving a coat of white on your cheek
That only a warm kiss or caress can erase.

Rural Collapse

Centurion oaks stand guard in sharp rows,
Protecting a lone white clapboard farm house
That is crumbling into the cellar below.
The property ceded now to raccoon and mouse
Who seek shelter from the rain, cold and snow;
And—when darkness punctures day—to carouse.
They raise their broods like homesteaders of old—
Unconcerned of what has been bought and sold.

Forgotten Field

The narrow path through the overgrown field
Was like a spinal chord from which every
Moment of his life branched out.
Every step involuntarily evoked memories
Of working the land with his father and brothers
When their muscles were granite and their
Limbs were as flexible as saplings.
Creaking like a rusty windmill, he was drawn
Back to his beginning and his end.
Clouds broke, revealing a bare summit that
Split the sky. He can no longer scramble
Up its rocky trails, but he remembered the feel
Of the sharp sun cutting through the cold at its peak.
He hoped that whomever owns this land in the
Future will send their offspring up the slope as
His father did. It will be their true baptism,
And, when the time comes, their true last rite.

Murder at Moon Lake

Living deep in the New Hampshire woods alone
Hardened Jim Osborne's heart like marble.
Suspicious of all of man's legal
Limits, he followed only nature's laws.
His rusting red Ford truck flew down hills
And around curves like a fox chasing a rabbit.
Officer Reynolds stopped him more than once.
Osborne laughed as tobacco juice spilled
Over his lips like a brown waterfall.
This cat-and-mouse game continued for years
Until Reynolds spotted the Ford truck
Parked after hours at Moon Lake.
The next morning, Reynolds lay dead next
To the truck; Osborne had bled out from
A shot to his groin and was discovered
In the dew-soaked woods.
The two men were buried at opposite
Ends of the town cemetery behind the
Congregational church. No one knew who
Had paid for Osborne's granite monument.
These things happen in small towns.

Severance Day

Demoralized and dated, he drove away
From the plant that provided his weekly pay
For thirty years, two mortgages, two children.
The severance pay was cool compensation
For arising each day and being a man—
Something only lunch-bucket heads understand.
He drifted home under an autumn copper sky,
Wondering if his wife could stifle a cry;
For mournful sobs were not what he needed now.
He craved to see a future out there somehow.

Ocean Light

He sat on the rocky shore of Maine—
His aspirations cauterized by age.
The flat sea that night was like polished granite;
Above the water stars boiled out of the darkness.
On the horizon he spotted a light.
He placed himself on the ship,
Heading toward Halifax or maybe Labrador.
Then the light slipped over the edge
Of the earth and disappeared.
He adjusted his cap and walked
To the nearest bar to drink three beers.

E Pluribus Unum

We were once one nation founded from the all;
This concept most people no longer recall.
Individual rights rule—it's understood.
What has been sacrificed is the common good.
Portfolios expand exponentially
For the privileged few who rule the country,
While the rest struggle and scrape to pay their debts.
These are the people government forgets.

Declaration

Ugliness I cannot tolerate;
This is my solemn declaration.

I have appealed to the highest magistrate
To release me from urban incarceration.

Transfer me to a valley where I can concentrate
On nature's magnification.

There will I find an end state
Where all is sublime simplification.

Marching In

March crept in furtively like a field mouse,
Slipping through small cracks in winter's house.
Bellicose winds once at winter's command
Surrendered subtlety to softer hands
That were not inclined to crack the cruel whip
Against the trees, which were pleased that the grip
Of their frigid master was loosening.
In the hard soil, flowers were aspiring
To inhale deep after holding their breath—
Their colors resurrected after death.
Why believe in myths and suspect stories;
Just kneel to worship to nature's glories.

Orchard in October

October light spilled over the orchard
Like baptismal water—blessed, sanctifying.
Twisting towers of smoke from burning leaves
Ascended softly—summer was dying.

Among the apples trees, an old man grasped
The ripe fruit with his mottled, crooked hand.
At the base of a rickety ladder
His granddaughter surveyed the wonderland

Of giant trees stretching to forever.
The old man looked into her wide blue eyes—
Pleased that her hands would one day pick
The fruit that ripens under Vermont skies.

William Graham

Place Setting

Winter set a full table
With characteristic flair.
Was I available
To attend the affair?

My answer was yes.
A tablecloth of white
Was laid down to impress.
The stars hung in the night

Sky like a chandelier.
Trees heavy with wet snow
Bent low to greet me there
In a frozen chateau.

The conversation lingered
As the heavens moved west.
In the east dawn stirred;
I left—a satisfied guest.

An Old Poet on Valentine's Day

The foundation of the stone house
Sagged like the old poet's jowls.
He had stopped noticing the mouse
Droppings on the floor or the owls
That had moved into the attic.
He spent his days dipping
Into verse from books that he picked
From wobbly shelves that were hanging
Precariously on rain-stained walls.
He scribbled blank verse on a yellow pad.
He stopped. He thought he heard the calls
Of the woman who had once driven him mad
With love. But she now sleeps with the divine.
He smiled while composing his last Valentine.

His Last Dance

He no longer looked upon his daughter—
But on a woman—at the wedding dance.
The girl who once held him in a deep trance
Would now fill another house with laughter.

How would he now measure his earthly worth?
He had nothing to nurture but himself.
"Pack me up gently for life on the shelf,"
He thought. "We start to die after our birth."

Down the drain he tossed his medications
That defined age. He started the engine,
Waiting for the long silence to begin—
Beatles tunes played on a sixties station.

Permanence

I sketched the fair face of my true love
With my glove after breathing onto the cold
Window pane of a bus in the bleak mid-winter.
But her silken cheeks and flaming eyes
Faded fast on the frost of the slush-caked glass.
Now my true love burrows beside me
Like a fox. Never more will I have to
Conjure her smile with my warm breath.

Adult Territory

Her body gleamed under an arc of moonlight
After the jungle frenzy of the night.
Inhibitions plundered by knowing hands,
She surrendered to his brilliant commands.
She would gladly again loosen the reins,
For the unutterable joy in her veins.
But she could sense the glitter would be gone
When the rumpled sheets met the damaged dawn.

Summer People

With a condo in Chicago,
And a large farm in Ohio.
Jim Andrews is building a house
In Sister Bay for his new spouse.

Retired from a career in bonds,
He is now being stretched beyond
What his portfolio can stand.
The beautiful piece of prime land

Nestled in pines along the shore
Cost him more than he bargained for.
But Chloe is limber and dear.
She wanted to summer this year.

The thought of her tan runner's limbs
In shorts always excited him—
And the way she poured adult drinks
After his sojourns on the links.

She has given him back purpose,
But he is not sure he can trust
Her unreservedly. Her eyes
Inspire other to seek the prize.

This would all be long forgotten,
For this smart summer they will spend
In Sister Bay—cool lake breezes;
He agreeing to all she says.

The Will

The family gathered in the sun-filled
Livingroom—waiting, wondering, silent.
Autumn's angled light sliced through the carpet.
Three sons and one daughter were not too thrilled

To be in the same room together after
Years of acrimony. The eldest sons
Had followed their patriarch on the throne
Of business—enlarging fortunes year

After year. Their younger brother and sister
Had chosen paths of endless excursions—
Parisian jaunts, exotic diversions
To locales here, there and everywhere.

A ceramic-faced lawyer read the will—
Equal legacies for all the children.
For two, it was now a matter of when
To file a contest. Their eyes caused wind chills

To hover below decent decorum
In such proceedings. The younger siblings
Smiled. They were already planning flings.
No work; just play and fanciful freedom.

The Mirror

While partaking of my morning shave,
I realized that the mirror was a grave.
Each delicate day grows more trying.
What's that sound? More neurons dying.
I can see all of the obvious signs—
The furrowed brown; the Grand Canyon face lines.
I inhale deeply; then blow out my breath
On the glass. One more day of cheating death!

THE POND

Tucked delicately in the woods of Maine—
Like a piece of grandmother's fine china—
Is Deception Pond. The locals maintain
That it has been cursed since young Regina

Hopewell's tragic demise in thirty-nine.
The winter that year was hard as iron.
"It is part of our God's sacred design,"
Faithful Regina, solid paragon

Of the churched, believed. After Sunday mass,
As the cold chewed through her hand-knit white scarf,
She crossed the pond—its ice clear as glass—
On her way to her aunt's. She felt dwarfed

As she stood in the center of the pond—
Enraptured by her God's grand creation.
The ice cracked. Her body was never found.
Now, no one walks on the pond called Deception.

Sunset Reflections

The sun gasped behind the trees
Of a park that overlooked the city
That sunk serenely into a pool of shadows.
She came here every evening to
Greet the birth of the night.
Her life looked less harsh enveloped
By the dark, she determined.
In the shadows could lurk possibilities
Instead of the harsh snap of the quotidian.
She lingered until the city glowed orange.
Then she shuffled off on the cold concrete—
Another day older.

The Four Elements: Love Poems

1.
Against the soft glow
Of a fire, her silhouette
Invited passion.

2.
Her long liquid limbs
Flowed through his raw hands like a
Cool mountain stream.

3.
Desperately, she
Floated like a coastal fog
Across wet scarred stones.

4.
Distant rolling hills
Receded in the distance
Like love forgotten.

Final Verse

His judgment was once as precise
As a Shakespearean sonnet.
People came to him for advice
And then they acted upon it.

His thoughts have lost classical rhyme.
He stoops instead of walking true.
He confuses places and time.
He scans the verse: it's death's prelude.

Made in the USA